Instant LEGO MINDSTORMS EV3

Your guide to building and programming your very own advanced robot using LEGO MINDSTORMS EV3

Gary Garber

PUBLISHING

BIRMINGHAM - MUMBAI

Instant LEGO MINDSTORMS EV3

First published: September 2013

Production Reference: 2291013

Published by Packt Publishing Ltd.
Livery Place
35 Livery Street
Birmingham B3 2PB, UK.

ISBN 978-1-84951-974-8

www.packtpub.com

Credits

Author
Gary Garber

Reviewers
Barbara Bratzel

Chris Rogers

Acquisition Editors
Owen Roberts

Jonathan Titmus

Commissioning Editor
Govindan K

Technical Editors
Manan Badani

Adrian Raposo

Project Coordinator
Akash Poojary

Proofreader
Lindsey Thomas

Graphics
Ronak Dhruv

Production Coordinator
Prachali Bhiwandkar

Cover Work
Prachali Bhiwandkar

Cover Image
Gary Garber

About the Author

Gary Garber teaches physics, math, and engineering at Boston University Academy. Gary is the Past-President of the New England Section of the American Association of Physics Teachers, and has led dozens of professional development workshops in education, on both the local and national level. Gary runs the Boston University FIRST Robotics program. He has run and hosted numerous robotics workshops in VEX, Tetrix, and LEGO platforms. He has also run several LEGO robotics tournaments and spoken on robotics education at both local and national conferences. His robotics team has worked with Engineers Without Borders, NASA, and the National Science Teachers Association on a variety of engineering and education projects. He is currently an educational consultant, working to develop new software tools for the classroom, at the Tufts Center for Engineering Education and Outreach, which is a pioneer in LEGO Robotics Education. He currently resides in Massachusetts, US and when he is not playing with LEGOS, robots, or toy trains, he enjoys spending time with his wife Catalina, and their two children, Alejandro and Leonardo.

I would like to thank the people of the Tufts Center for Engineering Education and Outreach for teaching me about LEGO robotics, and helping to make this book possible, including Chris Rogers, Ethan Danahy, Mary Theresa Nahill, Barbara Bratzle, Bill Church, and Leslie Schneider. I would also like to thank Steve Cremer and Craig Robinson for being my inspirations in the field of education.

About the Reviewers

Barbara Bratzel is a science teacher at the Shady Hill School in Cambridge, Massachusetts and a consulting teacher at the Center for Engineering Education and Outreach at Tufts University. In addition to teaching, she runs LEGO teacher workshops both in the United States and abroad. Her books include Physics by Design with NXT MINDSTORMS, Third Edition (2009) and LabVIEW Lessons: Classroom Activities for Learning and Using LabVIEW with LEGO MINDSTORMS (2011).

Chris Rogers got all three of his degrees at Stanford University, where he worked with John Eaton on his thesis looking at particle motion in a boundary layer flow. From Stanford, he went to Tufts as a faculty member, where he has remained since then, with a few exceptions. His first sabbatical was spent at Harvard, and a local kindergarten, looking at methods of teaching engineering. He spent half a year in New Zealand on a Fulbright Scholarship looking at the 3D reconstruction of flame fronts to estimate heat fluxes. In 2002-3, he was at Princeton, as the Kenan Professor of Distinguished Teaching, where he played with underwater robots, wind tunnels, and LEGO bricks. In 2006-7, he spent the year at ETH in Zurich, playing with very very small robots, and measuring the lift force on a fruit fly. He received the 2003 NSF Director's Distinguished Teaching Scholar Award for excellence in both teaching and research. Chris is involved in several different research areas: particle-laden flows (a continuation of his thesis), telerobotics and controls, slurry flows in chemical-mechanical planarization, the engineering of musical instruments, measuring flame shapes of couch fires, measuring fruit-fly locomotion, and elementary school engineering education. His work has been funded by numerous government organizations and corporations, including the NSF, NASA, Intel, Boeing, Cabot, Steinway, Selmer, National Instruments, Raytheon, Fulbright, and the LEGO Corporation. His work in particle-laden flows led to the opportunity to fly aboard the NASA 0g experimental aircraft. He has flown over 700 parabolas without getting sick.

Chris also has a strong commitment to teaching, and at Tufts has started a number of new directions, including learning robotics with LEGO bricks, and learning manufacturing by building musical instruments. He was awarded the Carnegie Professor of the Year in Massachusetts in 1998, and is currently the director of the Center for Engineering Education Outreach (`www.ceeo.tufts.edu`). His teaching work extends to elementary schools, where he talks with over 1000 teachers around the world every year, on ways of bringing engineering into the younger grades. He has worked with LEGO to develop ROBOLAB, a robotic approach to learning science and math. ROBOLAB has already gone into over 50,000 schools worldwide, and has been translated into 15 languages. He has been invited to speak on engineering education in Singapore, Hong Kong, Australia, New Zealand, Denmark, Sweden, Norway, Luxembourg, Switzerland, the UK, and in the US. He works in various classrooms once a week, although he has been banned from recess for making too much noise.

Most importantly, he has three kids—all brilliant, who are responsible for most of his research interests and efforts.

Chris is a professor at Tufts University, and his review in no way reflects the opinions of Tufts.

He has reviewed a number of fluid mechanics and robotics texts too.

www.PacktPub.com

Support files, eBooks, discount offers and more

You might want to visit www.PacktPub.com for support files and downloads related to your book.

Did you know that Packt offers eBook versions of every book published, with PDF and ePub files available? You can upgrade to the eBook version at www.PacktPub.com and as a print book customer, you are entitled to a discount on the eBook copy. Get in touch with us at service@packtpub.com for more details.

At www.PacktPub.com, you can also read a collection of free technical articles, sign up for a range of free newsletters and receive exclusive discounts and offers on Packt books and eBooks.

http://PacktLib.PacktPub.com

Do you need instant solutions to your IT questions? PacktLib is Packt's online digital book library. Here, you can access, read, and search across Packt's entire library of books.

Why Subscribe?

- ▶ Fully searchable across every book published by Packt
- ▶ Copy and paste, print, and bookmark content
- ▶ On demand and accessible via web browser

Free Access for Packt account holders

If you have an account with Packt at www.PacktPub.com, you can use this to access PacktLib today and view nine entirely free books. Simply use your login credentials for immediate access.

Table of Contents

Preface

LEGO bricks are high quality plastic parts made with precision moulds, which allow great versatility in design. The LEGO bricks in your MINDSTORMS kit consist of beams, gears, axles, pins, motors, and other sophisticated mechanical parts, allowing the user to construct elaborate contraptions with multiple moving parts. The brain of the MINDSTORMS EV3 is an intelligent brick, a programmable microcomputer, which contains an ARM9 processor running Linux. The EV3 can accept input from an array of electronic sensors, can link to a computer, and send output to motors, a speaker, or a built in color display screen. The programming language included with your kit is an easy to learn visual programming language.

This book is a practical guide to show you how to advance from the basic lessons included in your EV3 kit, combine the basic programming commands, and implement competition tested design principles in building a robot.

What this book covers

Building a robot (Simple) will help us to build and program a robot that moves with two drive wheels and a front castor. This robot will interact with its environment using a touch sensor and a motion sensor, and will use a small motor to move an arm.

Gyro sensor movement (Medium) will teach us to alter our robot, so that it navigates and makes turns using a gyro sensor. We will use programming commands such as loops, switches, MyBlocks, variables, and arrays.

Ultrasonic motion sensing (Advanced) will show us how to program our robot using a proportional algorithm, to allow greater precision in interacting with the environment. We will display information on the screen, and use the advanced math, loop interrupts, and read/write file programming commands.

Proportional line follower (Advanced) will teach us to alter our robot, so it can track a line using an optical sensor. We will use a proportional algorithm and adjust the parameters for optimum tracking. Finally, we will also write a program allowing the robot to be calibrated without the use of a computer.

What you need for this book

For this book you will need the LEGO MINDSTORMS Education EV3 set. If your set does not include a motion sensor, you will need that too. You will also need the LEGO brand EV3 software.

Who this book is for

This book is for both the adult tinkerer who has never touched LEGOS before, and the experienced LEGO enthusiast who has evolved from the MINDSTORMS NXT to the EV3. If you are interested in entering or advising students in robot competitions, such as the FIRST LEGO League, the World Robot Olympiad, or RoboGames, this book is a must for you. Even if you haven't purchased your MINDSTORMS EV3 kit yet, this book will give you a good introduction to the platform.

Conventions

In this book, you will find a number of styles of text that distinguish between different kinds of information. Here are some examples of these styles, and an explanation of their meaning.

New terms and **important words** are shown in bold. Words that you see on the screen, in menus or dialog boxes for example, appear in the text like this: "Next click on the **Download and Run** button".

Reader feedback

Feedback from our readers is always welcome. Let us know what you think about this book— what you liked or may have disliked. Reader feedback is important for us to develop titles that you really get the most out of.

To send us general feedback, simply send an e-mail to feedback@packtpub.com, and mention the book title via the subject of your message.

If there is a topic that you have expertise in and you are interested in either writing or contributing to a book, see our author guide on www.packtpub.com/authors.

Customer support

Now that you are the proud owner of a Packt book, we have a number of things to help you to get the most from your purchase.

Downloading the example code

You can download the example code files for all Packt books you have purchased from your account at http://www.packtpub.com. If you purchased this book elsewhere, you can visit http://www.packtpub.com/support and register to have the files e-mailed directly to you.

Downloading the color images of this book

We also provide you a PDF file that has color images of the screenshots/diagrams used in this book. The color images will help you better understand the changes in the output. You can download this file from `http://www.packtpub.com/sites/default/files/downloads/9748OT_Graphics.pdf`.

Errata

Although we have taken every care to ensure the accuracy of our content, mistakes do happen. If you find a mistake in one of our books—maybe a mistake in the text or the code—we would be grateful if you would report this to us. By doing so, you can save other readers from frustration and help us improve subsequent versions of this book. If you find any errata, please report them by visiting `http://www.packtpub.com/submit-errata`, selecting your book, clicking on the **errata submission form** link, and entering the details of your errata. Once your errata are verified, your submission will be accepted and the errata will be uploaded on our website, or added to any list of existing errata, under the Errata section of that title. Any existing errata can be viewed by selecting your title from `http://www.packtpub.com/support`.

Piracy

Piracy of copyright material on the Internet is an ongoing problem across all media. At Packt, we take the protection of our copyright and licenses very seriously. If you come across any illegal copies of our works, in any form, on the Internet, please provide us with the location address or website name immediately so that we can pursue a remedy.

Please contact us at `copyright@packtpub.com` with a link to the suspected pirated material.

We appreciate your help in protecting our authors, and our ability to bring you valuable content.

Questions

You can contact us at `questions@packtpub.com` if you are having a problem with any aspect of the book, and we will do our best to address it.

Instant LEGO MINDSTORMS EV3

Welcome to *Instant LEGO MINDSTORMS EV3*!

At the end of this book you will be able to build and program the new LEGO MINDSTORMS EV3 to interact with its surroundings. The EV3 will be able to navigate around obstacles, track a crooked line, and maintain its distance from a moving object. You will also learn how to use several sensors with proportional control algorithms.

The EV3 kit contains hundreds of pieces of LEGO bricks. LEGO bricks are high quality plastic parts made with precision moulds, which allow great versatility in the design of robots. The classic LEGO brick was created with a modular spacing that hasn't changed in decades. Because of superior quality and manufacturing processes, the parts I played with, 40 years ago as a boy are fully compatible with the parts made today. The kit contains Technic LEGO bricks consisting of beams, gears, axles, and pins. The EV3 Intelligent Brick contains an ARM9 processor which operates with a Linux based operating system. The EV3 Intelligent Brick has an SDHC Card reader that allows us to make full use of the Linux OS. The extra USB port enables Wi-Fi communication with a dongle. The motors have built-in shaft encoders. Available LEGO sensors include gyro sensors, IR sensors, ultrasonic motion sensors, color sensors, and touch sensors.

LEGO, in collaboration with National Instruments, has developed its own EV3 software which is a visual programming language. The EV3 software is based on **LabVIEW (Laboratory Virtual Instrument Engineering Workbench)**, a visual programming language which is used throughout science, and engineering fields to control instrumentation. LabVIEW is used on probes sent to Mars, to control the world's largest particle accelerator, CERN, and at almost every university in the world for data acquisition and control. When I was first introduced to computer science, I initially described the concept of my programs with a flow chart. LabVIEW and EV3 make this flow chart into an actual programming language. Instead of statements or lines of code, EV3 uses blocks connected by wires representing the flow of data.

Because of the Linux OS, we are able to program the EV3 Intelligent Brick in numerous languages. Other than EV3, the most common languages are **RobotC** and LabVIEW. I have written this version of the book for the EV3 programming languages and because of the visual nature, it excels at running parallel threads. Most third-party sensor vendors have written downloads for their sensors in EV3, RobotC, NXC, and LabVIEW. In EV3, the downloads are called "MyBlocks", which is the LEGO term for a subroutine. Another advantage of visual language programming is that you can view your entire program at once. When running the debugger, you can actually view which step of the program your robot is executing in real time. Throughout this book we will explore all of the main programming algorithms for programming LEGO robots, including subroutines, loops, if-then statements, variables, constants, and operators. The EV3 language also has a great "scratch page" feature that allows for extensive annotation of the code including videos and images.

The robot in this book is designed with simplicity, balance, and versatility in mind. When I introduce my own students to robotics, I often have them study and/or build complex robots following instructions. I would encourage you to build several of the plans included in your LEGO EV3 set. By following the kit instructions provided by LEGO for over a dozen robots, you will gain a solid introduction to using pins, beams, gears, and motors for building robots. One of the best things about making robots from LEGO is that it allows solution diversity. Over the past 15 years, I have coached students in building dozens of robots with LEGO, TETRIX, VEX, and FIRST platforms. However when designing a robot from scratch, I encourage students to follow the **KISS** (**Keep It Simple Stupid**) approach, which I used in the robot design included in this book. You should be able to build the base robot in less than 12 minutes.

By the end of this book you will be familiar with using a proportional controller. In our daily lives, we are surrounded by on-off controllers such as thermostats. Many controllers, such as cruise control on a car, are proportional. The farther you are from your desired speed, the stronger the car will react. When we see a stop sign, our own reactions with the brake pedal are proportional to how far we are from that stop sign and our current speed.

Building a robot (Simple)

You will build a basic robot with two drive wheels and one manipulator. This robot will be easily customizable with many sensors. It will sense and interact with its surroundings. The robot will move towards a wall, touch the wall, and move its arm. You will find that you can easily modify this design and create your own unique robot.

Getting ready

We will first need to gather the following parts from your EV3 set. The parts include several beams, pins, axles, your EV3 Intelligent Brick, two large motors, and some wires. The parts that we will need are shown in the next figure:

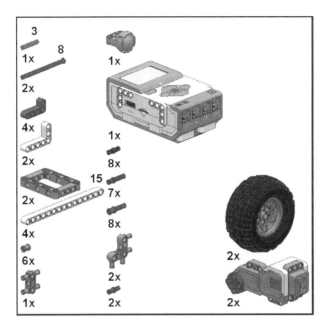

You will need to charge up the battery included in your kit or install six AA batteries. You will also need to install the EV3 software on your computer.

How to do it...

We will follow these step by step instructions to build the robot:

1. Start with your EV3 Intelligent Brick which is shown in the next figure:

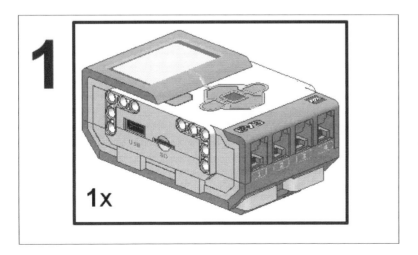

2. Flip your brick over and attach four black friction pins as shown in the next figure:

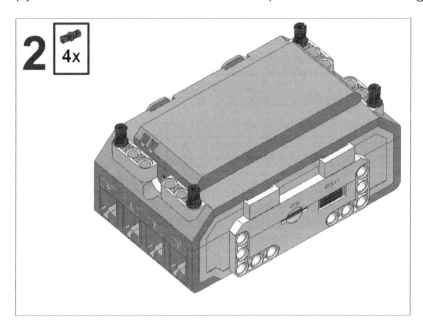

3. Place two white 15 module long beams onto the pins. A module is the unit of length of LEGO bricks and is the spacing between studs on the bricks as shown in the next figure:

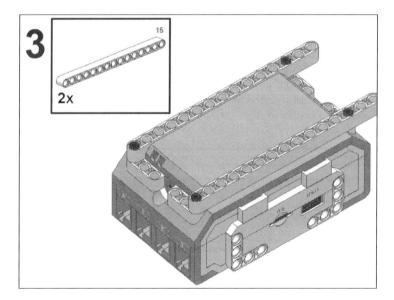

4. We will now add four long blue pins, two black pins, and two more beams as shown in the next figure:

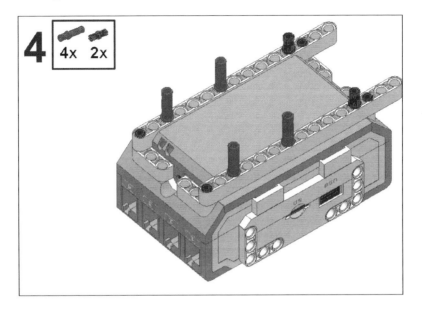

5. Make sure that the short end of the blue pins are facing the brick as you can see in the next figure:

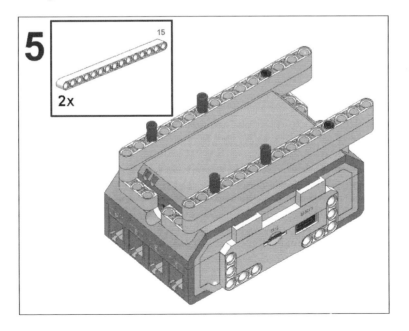

6. You will now join two open frame beams with a cross block which forms the chassis of your robot. Building this sub-assembly is broken up into three steps as shown in the next figure:

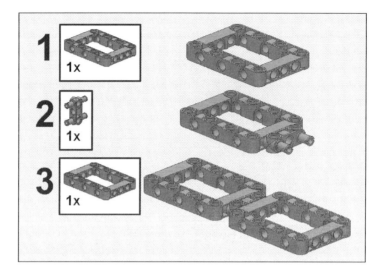

7. Place the chassis onto the bottom of your robot as shown in the next figure:

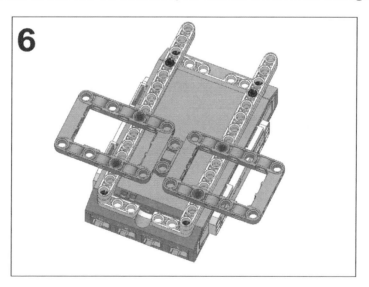

8. Next, we are going to build an assembly to hold the caster wheel. You will need the perpendicular connector pin, the caster, a 3-module axle, two red 2x4 bent beams, and a long blue pin. This assembly is divided up into four steps as shown in the next figure:

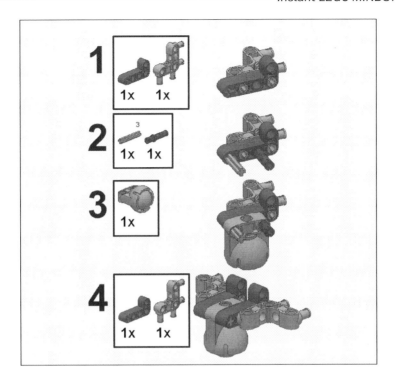

9. Attach the caster assembly onto the chassis as shown in the next figure:

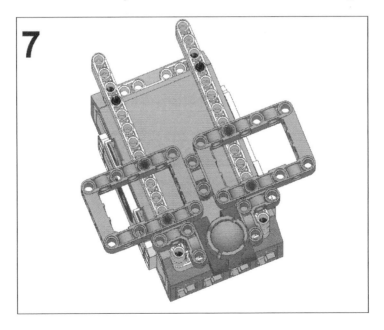

10. Now we are going to build the right-hand motor assembly. There will be six steps to build the motor assembly. To begin, combine a motor, an 8-module stop-axle, and two bushings as shown in the next figure:

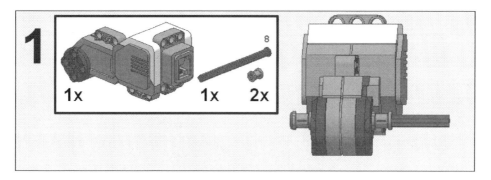

11. Attach a hub and tire to the axle as shown in the next figure:

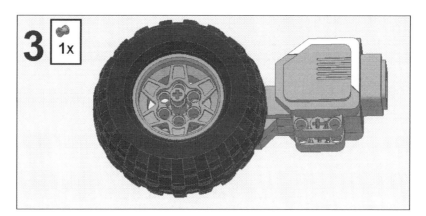

12. To secure the tire, place a bushing on the end of the axle as shown in the next figure:

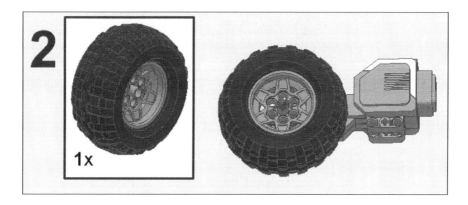

13. Insert a blue long pin and a blue axle pin into the motor as shown in the next figure:

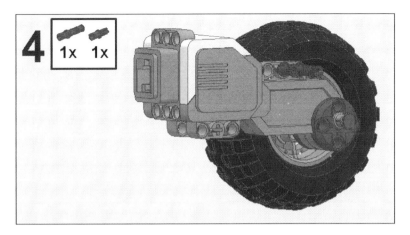

14. Attach a black pin and red 2x4 bent beam as shown in the next figure:

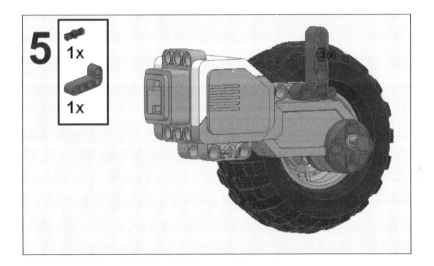

15. Attach a white 3x5 bent beam as shown in the next figure:

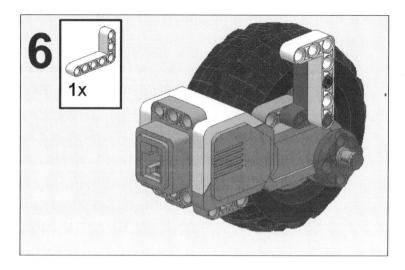

16. Attach the right motor assembly to your robot, with four red long pins with stop bushings as shown in the next figure:

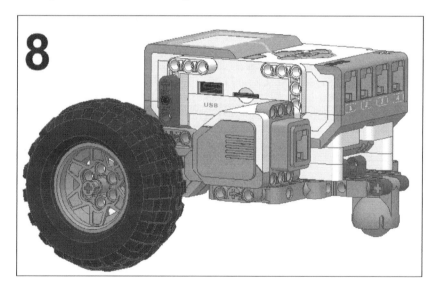

17. In the next figure you can see the location of the four red stop bushings:

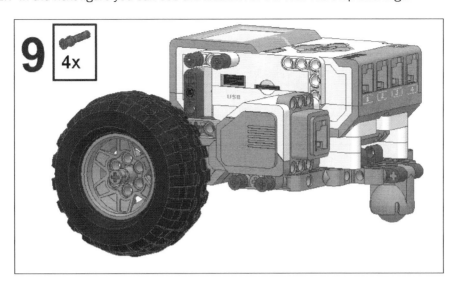

18. Now we will repeat the entire process for the left-hand motor assembly as shown in the next figure:

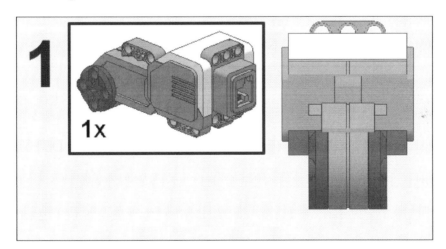

19. Combine a motor, an 8-module stop-axle, and two bushings as shown in the next figure:

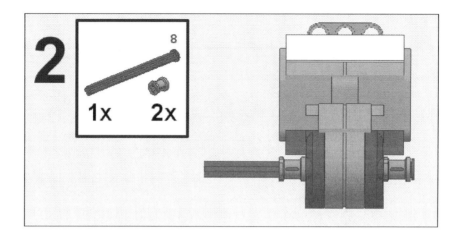

20. Attach a hub and a tire to the axle. To secure the tire, place a bushing on the end of the axle as shown in the next figure:

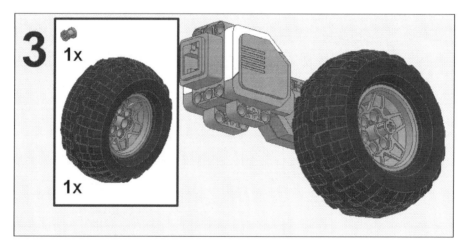

21. Insert a blue long pin and a blue axle pin into the motor as shown in the next figure:

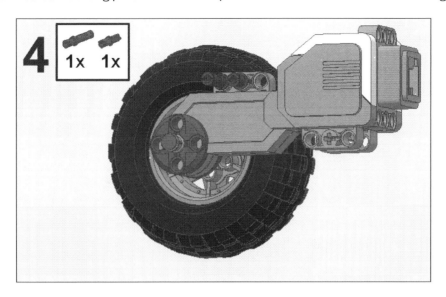

22. Attach a black pin and red 2x4 bent beam as shown in the next figure:

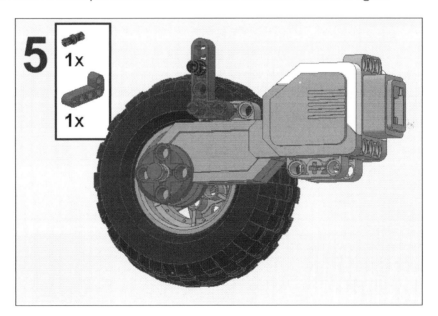

23. Attach a white 3x5 bent beam as shown in the next figure:

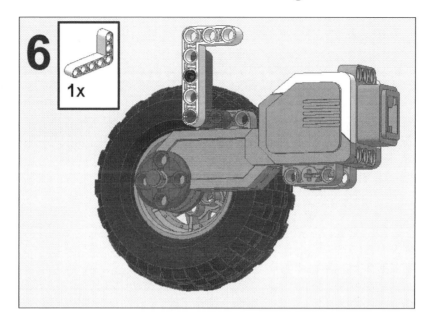

24. Attach the right motor assembly to your robot with four red long pins with stop bushings as shown in the next figure:

25. In the next figure you can see the location of the four red stop bushings as shown:

After attaching wires, our robot will be ready for a test drive. Connect the left-hand motor to Port C on your EV3 brick. Connect the right-hand motor to Port B on your EV3 brick. Turn on your EV3 brick by pressing the dark gray button in the center of the brick.

When you run the EV3 software:

1. We are going to write a program to make the robot move forward. Navigate to **File | New Project | Program** as shown in the next screenshot. This will start up a new program. You could easily start one of the many LEGO tutorials at this point, or perform data logging with an experiment. We will start with a blank sheet.

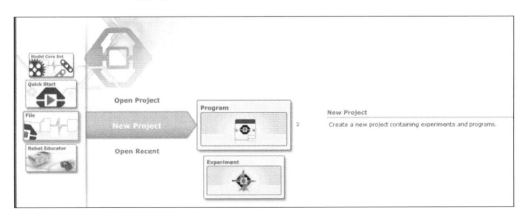

2. You will see several icons at the bottom of the screen on the Programming Palette as shown in the next screenshot:

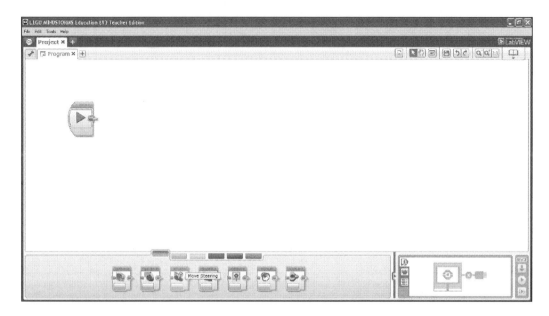

3. Drag a `Move Steering` block onto the Programming Canvas and place it next to the `Start` block as shown in the next screenshot:

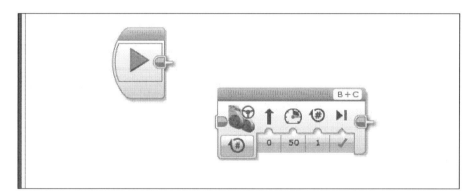

4. Using the drop-down menu, set the `Move Steering` block to **On for Rotations**. Set the **#** of rotations of the wheels to 5 as shown in the next screenshot. The motors have built-in shaft encoders which can tell how far they have rotated. The direction can be set to zero, which is straight ahead. The power level can be set to 50 percent. The motors are set to ports B and C.

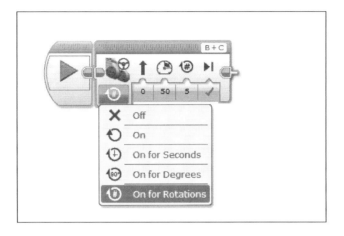

5. Although not required, you can set a `Stop` block at the end of the program. Make sure your robot is connected to your computer via the USB cable. You could also connect via Bluetooth. Next, click on the **Download and Run** button. Your robot should now move backward! You can also run it by clicking on the run icon as shown in the next screenshot:

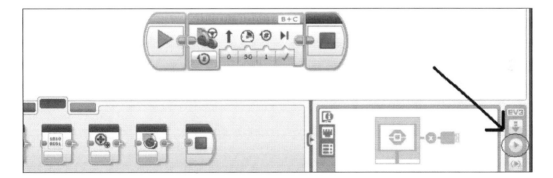

How it works...

The robot in this book has a very low center of gravity to prevent tipping. We need this added stability if your robot is going to climb ramps or use an extended arm. One of the greatest features to the medium strength motor is its weight. It is difficult to place large motors high up on your robot without tipping. I have placed the powered drive wheels in the rear with the caster and sensors in the front to allow a quicker response time to the environment. The base robot is simple to build and should be quick to modify for your own designs.

There's more...

We will now attach sensors and program the robot to interact with its environment using those sensors.

Attaching the sensors

In the next set of steps we will add a touch sensor, a medium size motor, and an ultrasonic motion sensor:

1. We will now attach sensors and a medium size motor to the parts of our robot seen in the next figure:

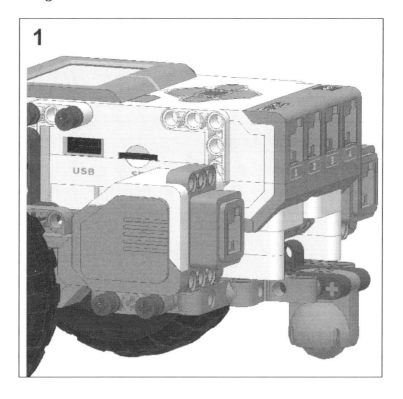

2. Insert two black pins on the right side of the robot in order to attach the touch sensor as shown in the next figure:

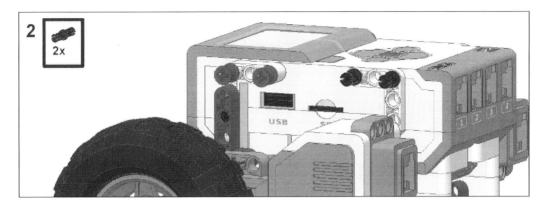

3. Attach the touch sensor as shown in the next figure. You can connect the touch sensor to Port 1 with a wire. You can insert an axle of any length into the touch sensor. Any gear on the end of the axle will make it easier for the sensor to touch things.

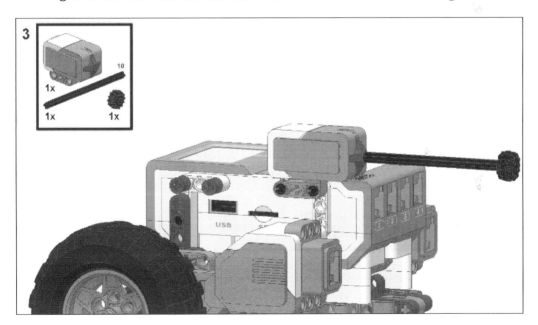

4. Now we will attach a medium size motor as a manipulator. Insert a perpendicular connector pin into the right-side motor as shown in the next figure:

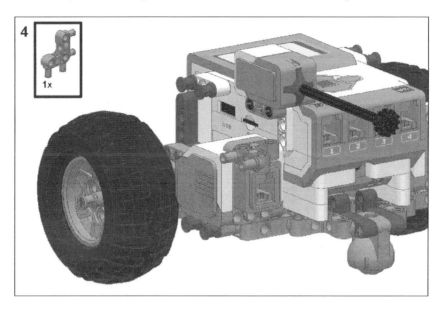

5. Insert two black pins into the connector pin as shown in the next figure:

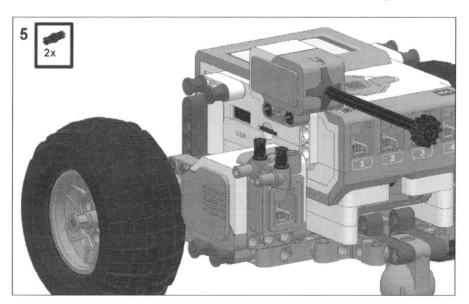

6. Attach the medium size motor to the two black pins as shown in the next figure:

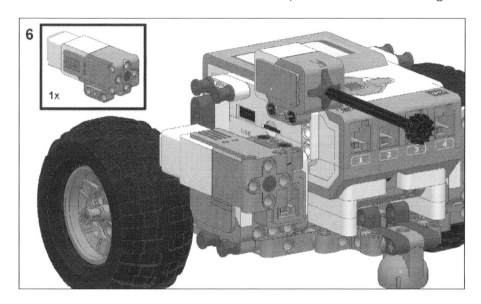

7. Insert an axle into the medium size motor. Slide a cross block onto the axle, and insert three black pins into the cross block as shown in the next figure:

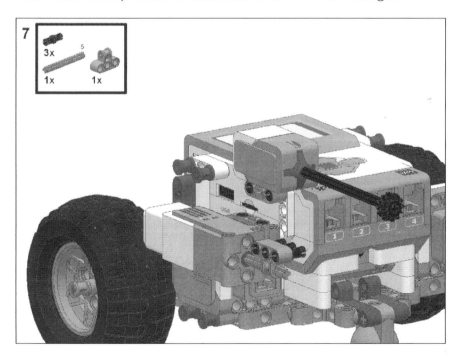

8. Attach three gray beams (11 modules long) to the assembly. Insert a black pin into each beam as shown in the next figure:

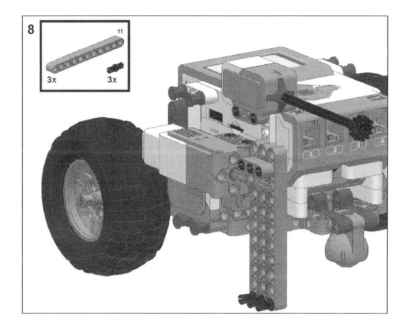

9. Attach a beam to the pins to act as a toe for kicking as shown in the next figure. Your robot is now ready to kick small objects. The motor can be wired to Port A.

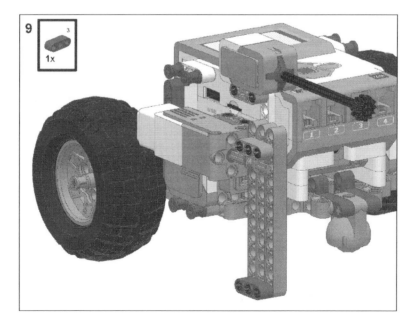

10. Next, we will attach an ultrasonic motion sensor. Insert two black pins onto the left side of the robot as shown in the next figure:

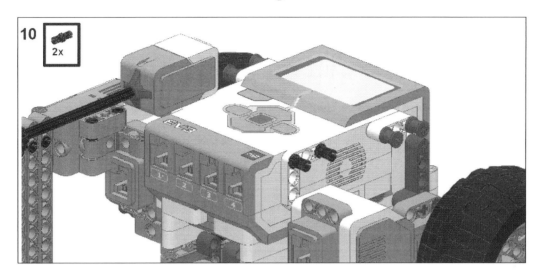

11. Attach the motion sensor onto the black pins. Connect the motion sensor to Port 2 with a wire as shown in the next figure:

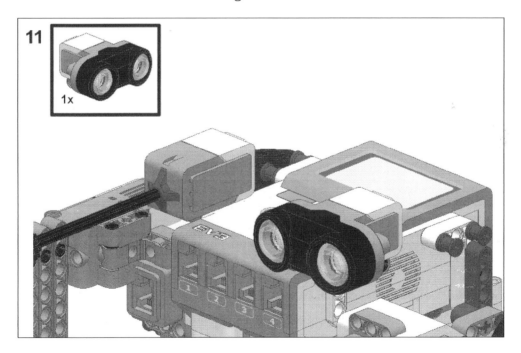

Using wires and wait block

In the following program, the robot will move forward, pause for one second and honk its horn. The Move Steering block moves the robot forward for one rotation of the wheels at 20 percent power. The Wait block will wait for a timing signal of one second. The Sound block can play tones or music from a file. This block will play a tone at 440 Hz for one second at full volume. The next, Move Steering block runs the motors at 100 percent power until signaled to shut down. The next Wait block will wait for a change in signal from the touch sensor. The EV3 will auto-ID the sensors and can tell that the touch sensor is connected to Port 1 if the sensor is plugged in before you place the block on the Programming Canvas. Although the first six blocks are connected by touching each other, you can also connect the blocks with wires as you would for a real instrument. If you click on the Sequence Plug Exit of a block, a wired space between blocks will open up. You can drag this wire to the next command block. This also allows you to make your code two dimensional. One important aspect of visual programming is being able to view your entire code on the screen at one time. These events are illustrated in the following screenshot:

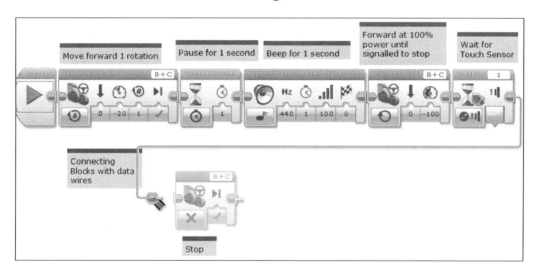

You can also split the wires to run parallel threads in your program. In this case, the wires run to both the `Medium Motor` block and the `Move Steering` block. The `Medium Motor` block will move the kicker foot on our robot for 0.5 seconds at 31 percent power. The `Move Steering` block will back our robot up for 3 seconds.

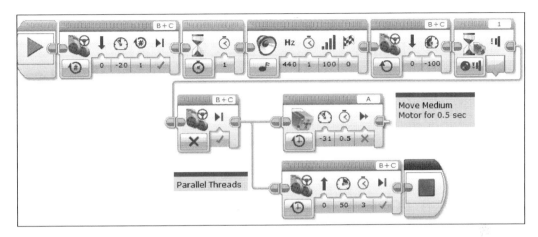

Ultrasonic motion sensor

We will now use the ultrasonic motion sensor to trigger a command in the program. We can set the ultrasonic sensor to measure distances or to listen to sudden sounds. In this case, we will set the `Wait` block to measure a distance less than 25 centimeters. In the lower right hand corner of the following screenshot, you can see that EV3 detects the motors in the Ports B and C and the motion sensor in Port 2.

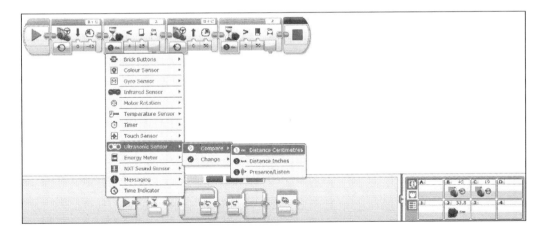

This program will make the robot move forward with a `Move Steering` block until a signal from the `Wait` block. The `Wait` block is triggered by an object at 25 cm. The next `Move Steering` block will move the robot in reverse until the next `Wait` block. The next `Wait` block is triggered when the motion sensor reads 50 cm as shown in the following screenshot:

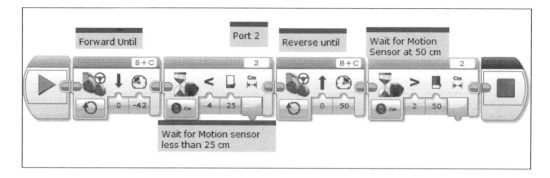

Medium size motor

Using a combination of the touch sensor and ultrasonic sensor the robot can stop when it hits the wall, and then back up 25 cm and stop. Then the robot can kick a ball with its medium motor assembly as shown in the following screenshot:

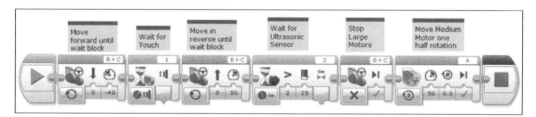

Gyro sensor movement (Medium)

Using the gyro sensor, the robot will move in a series of motions to follow a square or avoid an obstacle.

Getting ready

The following steps explain how to attach the gyro sensor to our robot:

1. First, take two axles which are three modules long with stops and attach them to the gyro sensor with bushings as shown in the following figure:

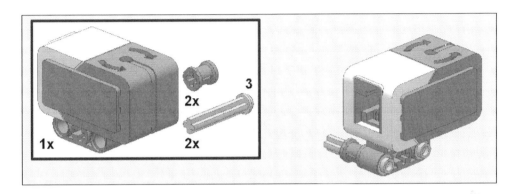

2. Next, we will attach the gyro sensor to the two red stop bushings on the back of the robot. We can wire the gyro sensor to Port 4 on our EV3 brick.

How to do it...

Make the robot go forward, turn until the gyro says it has turned 90 degrees, go forward, and repeat this sequence several times.

1. We will first use a Loop Flow block and select the COUNT mode for the loop block. We can make the robot repeat this turning sequence several times.

2. Inside this loop the robot will move forward for one rotation of the wheels.

3. Move while steering until the Wait block is triggered by a change in state of the gyro sensor by 90 degrees.

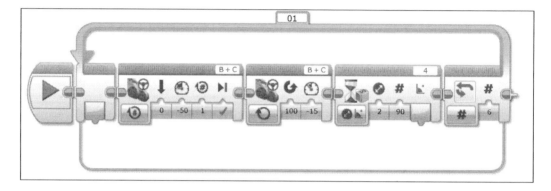

4. Before you run the program, you need to make sure that the robot is stationary. It is critical to reset the gyro sensor by unplugging it and plugging it back in while the robot is stationary. We can now run this program. If you notice that your gyro values keep changing even though the robot is not moving, this means the gyro needs to be reset.

How it works...

The gyro sensor detects rotational motion. You can use it to measure the angle or the angular speed. Using the gyro sensor will allow you to quickly make accurate turns. Without a gyro sensor, you would have to navigate using a technique called dead reckoning. This consists of mapping the turning of your robot by using the build-in shaft encoders on the wheels.

The gyro will drift over time, so it is a good idea to reset the gyro when using it in your programs. Including both a Reset Gyro block and unplugging the hardware are good ideas when using the gyro sensor.

There's more...

You will notice that using this simple code, the robot does not make a perfect square. This is because you are asking the robot to stop exactly at the 90 degree signal, by which time it is too late because of the inertia of the robot. In the remaining recipes, we will optimize the motion of the robot and program the robot to steer around obstacles.

Loop Index and Switches

To diagnose why the robot is not turning in a perfect square, we will alter our previous program by making the robot display on the screen what angle the gyro is currently reading. First, start out by clearing the EV3 display screen with a `Display` block. Make sure you set the `Display` block to `Text` and replace the word **MINDSTORMS** with an empty space. This is followed by the `Reset Gyro` block. Inside the loop, add a `Move` block set to stop, and a `Wait` block (for 2 seconds) to allow you time to read the angle. Place a `Display` block set to Text Grid mode with the Erase input unselected. Draw a wire from the Angle output of the `Wait Gyro` block to the Text input of the `Display` block. Although the `Wait` block is acting upon changes in 90 degrees, it will send the actual angle measurement. The displayed text will overlap. We can control the placement of text on the screen using the index counter of our loop. Create a `Math` block which will multiply numbers by 2. Run a wire from the `Loop Index` block to the `Math` block. Run a wire from the output of the `Math` block to the Y-coordinate input of the `Display` block. As the loop runs through subsequent iterations, the index increases and so will the placement of text on the display screen. This process is illustrated in the following screenshot:

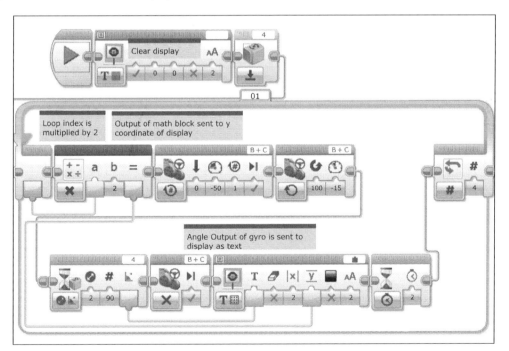

When you look at the numbers on the brick display, you will find that on each turn, the robot is overshooting the turn. This is because the robot does not begin stopping until it reaches 90 degrees. And as it overshoots each turn, these errors build on each other to create a path which is anything but a perfect square.

We will now use a `case` structure to add a correction to the turns. In the EV3 language, a `case` structure, or `if-then` statement is called a Switch Flow block. The Switch can be controlled by the sensors' other logic statements. Although you typically will have only two cases, you could add several other branches to the case structure. Each branch of the switch is called a `case` statement and can consist of several programming blocks. We will use the gyro sensor to define the case to try and *zigzag* onto the exact 90 degree angle. In the next screenshot you can see the entire code:

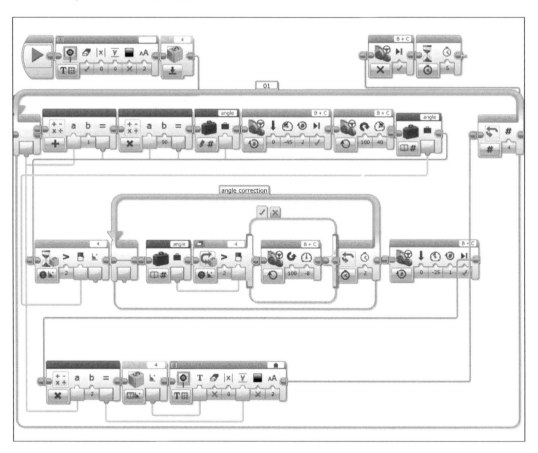

Initially, we asked the gyro sensor to wait only when it had turned 90 degrees on each leg of our square. Now we will adjust our code to ask the robot to stop turning when it reaches 90, 180, 270, and 360 degrees. We will do this by using a `Variable` block set to write numeric mode. We will give this `Variable` block the name `Angle`. The index counter on the loop runs through the sequence 0, 1, 2, and 3. We will use two math functions to come up with these degrees. Run a wire from the `Index Counter` block to a `Math` block set to math mode and add 1 to each number. The output of the add `Math` block should go to a `Math` block set to multiply mode. This number should be multiplied by 90 and the output should be sent to the `Variable` block. After the `Move Steering` block, the `Wait Gyro` block will be triggered when the sensor reads an angle greater than the `Variable` block as shown in the following screenshot:

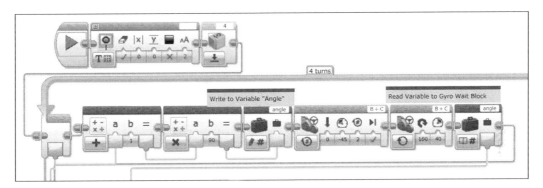

This brings us to the `Switch` block. The `Switch` block will have two cases defined by readings from the gyro sensor. If the gyro sensor has a reading greater than the output of the `Variable` block, it will follow Case 1, which contains a `Move Steering` block, which is set to the left. If the gyro sensor has a reading less than or equal to the output of the `Variable` block, it will follow Case 2, which contains a `Move Steering` block, which is set to the right.

We will allow this correction to repeat itself several times by placing it inside a `Loop Flow` block which will repeat the decision making for two seconds. The result will be a zigzag motion approaching the exact angle as shown in the following screenshot:

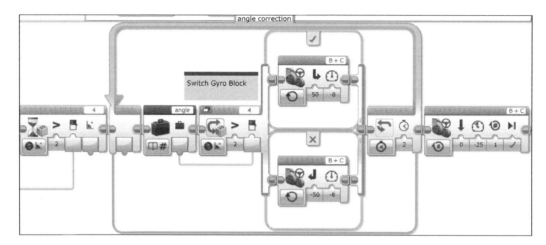

The previous screenshot has an expanded view showing both cases of the switch. You can also use a tabbed view of the switch. The next screenshot shows the positive case:

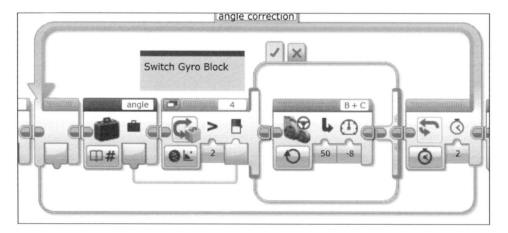

The next screenshot shows the negative case of the switch:

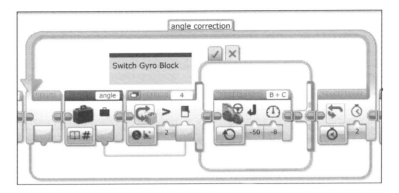

We are using a somewhat logic based decision to turn and hoping to get as close as possible, which gives a chaotic zigzag motion. We should use a proportional algorithm, which would slow the robot down as it approaches 90 degrees. We will explore proportional algorithms in the *Ultrasonic motion sensing* recipe.

MyBlocks

In this section we will program the robot to move forward until it encounters an unknown obstacle with the touch sensor and then attempt to steer around the obstacle. An obstacle such as a table or chair leg would be ideal. We will program the robot to take input from the brick buttons. The program we will initially write is inefficient and repetitive. It is actually a good example of how you shouldn't write a program. Remember, you should be able to view your entire code all at once. We will simplify the code using the EV3 version of a subroutine called `MyBlock`.

We will start a new program by resetting the gyro sensor. The robot will then move forward until the `Wait` block is triggered by a change in the state of the touch sensor. We will then program the robot to move back for one rotation of the wheels and display the following message onto the brick screen **Press left or right**. The next `Wait` block will wait for the user to press one of the brick buttons on the EV3 brick. This will be followed by a case structure or the `Switch Flow` block as shown in the following screenshot:

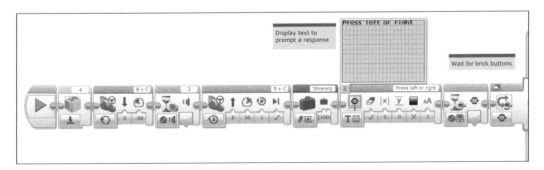

The Switch Flow block has two cases, one if the left brick button is depressed, and the other if the right brick button is depressed. The user will determine if they want the robot to avoid the obstacle by taking a detour to the left or right of the obstacle. Each case structure contains eleven blocks. The robot turns until triggered by the gyro, moves, turns, moves, and so on. The sequence is so long, that we cannot even view the entire code on one screen:

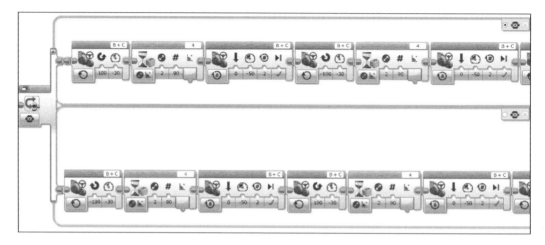

Here is the second part of the code:

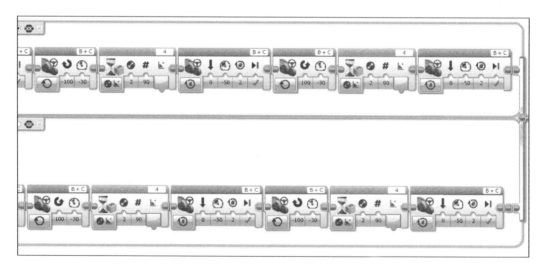

At this point, we can download and execute the code and the robot should be able to steer around a small rigid object.

We can now simplify the code using a MyBlock or a subroutine. Select all of the blocks inside one branch of the case structure. You will know the blocks have been selected because they will be highlighted with a light blue perimeter. Then, under the **Tools** drop-down menu select **My Block Builder**:

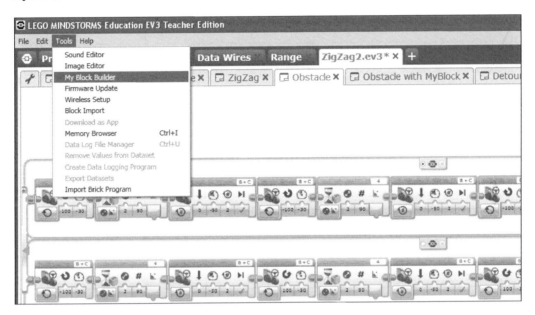

The **My Block Builder** screen (as shown in the previous screenshot) will pop up and ask you to name the MyBlock which is akin to naming a subroutine. You can also write a description and select an icon. You can also design an icon. You might also notice that the MyBlock can be modified to accept parameters. For our first introduction to the MyBlock, we will just use it to simplify the code. In the *Ultrasonic motion sensing* recipe, we will cover MyBlocks in more detail. We will name this MyBlock, LEFT.

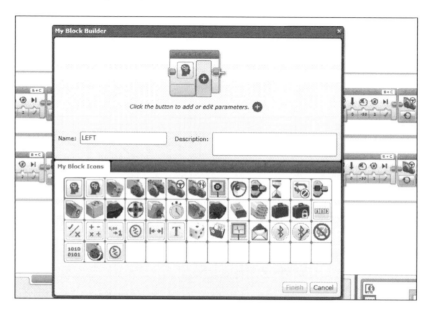

You should do the same for the other branch of the case structure (or switch), but instead, name that MyBlock, RIGHT. After you have defined a MyBlock, you can find it in the Programming Palette under the commands in the light blue programming blocks tab which you can see at the bottom of the next screenshot:

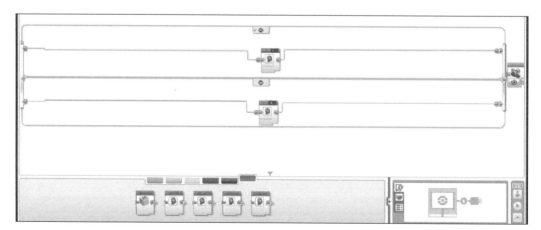

At this point, we can clean up the code by deleting a lot of the empty space which has been created inside the `Switch` block. We can now download and execute this simplified code:

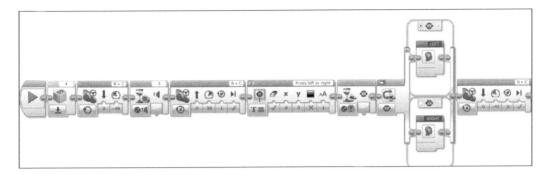

Arrays

In the previous section, we saw how to simplify the program to avoid an obstacle using a MyBlock (subroutine). In this section, we will optimize the program using an array instead. To learn how an array in EV3 works, we will first write a program to display a series of numbers on the EV3 brick screen.

First, clear the display screen. Then define a variable called `Steering`. Instead of writing to a numeric variable, we are going to write to an array. The difference between a variable and an array is that a variable only contains one value or element, whereas an array can contain several values or elements. This is illustrated in the following screenshot:

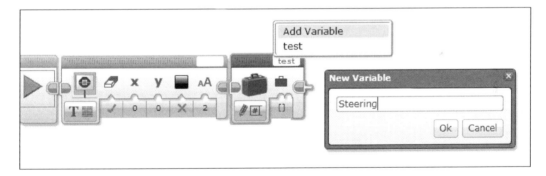

We will write the series of numbers [100, -100, -100, 100] into the array as shown in the following screenshot. This will be useful later when we use this same write variable block in the obstacle code.

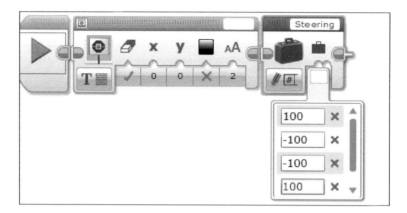

We will now create a loop called Display Steering which will repeat four times. The first block in our loop will be the read array variable block. It will then send via a wire the information from the variable steering block into an array operation block. We will also run a wire from the loop index into the array operation. This will allow us to read a different element in the array every iteration of the loop. This element will be sent as text to the display screen via a wire. Remember to uncheck that the display will not erase each time it runs. Again, the Y-coordinate location on the display screen is increased by a multiple of the loop index. When you run this program, you should see the elements of the array displayed in a column on the brick screen every two seconds. This is illustrated in the following screenshot:

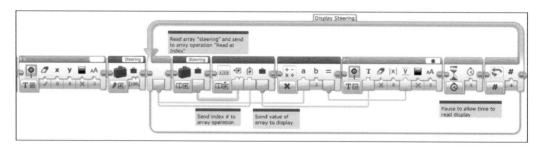

Now we are going to use an array to modify the obstacle code we wrote in the previous section. You will need to add the `write array` variable block in the beginning of the program before the case structure.

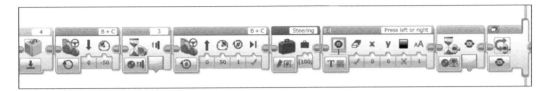

Replace the code you had previously written in the left button case structure with the following blocks. First, place a loop which will run for 4 counts into the case structure. Next, send the output from a `read array variable` block to an `array operation` block. Also, run a wire from the `loop index` block to the `array operation` block. We will run a wire from the `array operation` block output to the `move steering` block direction input. The array is telling the robot which direction to turn. Remember, the array contains the elements [`100`, `-100`, `-100`, `100`]. If the program chooses the first or last elements, then the steering value is to the left. If the program chooses the second or third elements, then the steering value is to the right. During each loop, the element which is chosen is determined by `loop index`. The robot will turn until the `Wait Gyro` block reaches 90 degrees. The robot will then move forward for two rotations of the wheels and the loop will repeat. This is illustrated in the following screenshot:

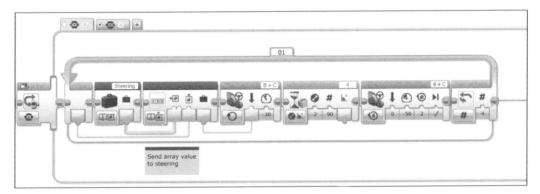

The other side of the case structure (resulting when the right button is pushed) has a similar code. We can modify the direction of the robot by adding a `Math` block, which will send the opposite value of the array elements to the `Move Steering` block. This is illustrated in the following screenshot:

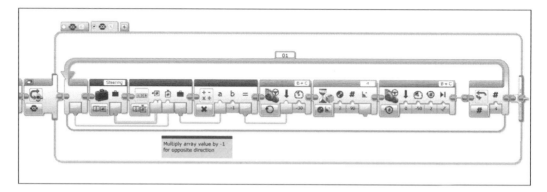

We will find that it is possible to view the entire optimized program on one screen:

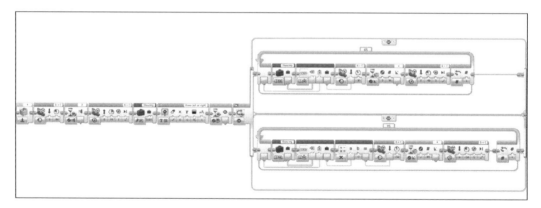

Ultrasonic motion sensing (Advanced)

In this recipe, we will program the robot to gradually come to a stop using a proportional algorithm. We will also use some more advanced programming blocks such as advanced math, MyBlocks, and writing to datafiles.

Getting ready

Make sure you have your motion sensor attached to the robot with a wire plugging the motion sensor into Port 2.

How to do it...

We are going to start out with some simple code and gradually add complexity to it. As a reminder, let us reexamine some code similar to what we wrote in the *Building a robot* recipe. In this code, the robot moves forward until the `Wait` block tells it to stop 25 cm from a wall.

1. Write, download, and execute this code as shown in the next screenshot:

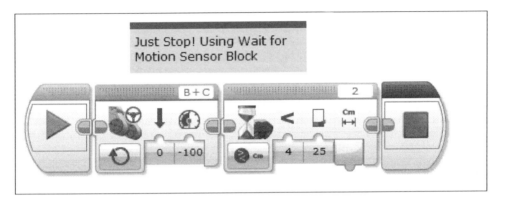

As you can see, the robot begins to stop 25 cm from the wall, but cannot stop immediately. To do this, the robot will need to slow down before it gets to the stopping point.

2. In the next set of code, we create a loop called `Slow Down`. Inside this loop, readings from the Ultrasonic Motion Sensor block are sent to a `Math` block (to take the negative of the position values) and then sent to the Power input of a `Move Steering` block. We can have the loop end when it reaches our desired stopping distance as shown in the next screenshot. Execute this code.

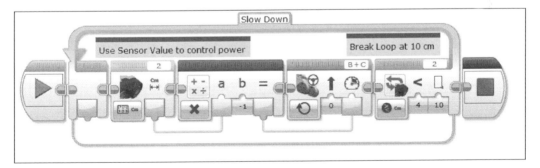

3. Instead of using the raw values, we can use the difference between the actual position and the desired position to control the `Move Steering` block as shown in the next screenshot. The power is actually proportional to the difference between the positions. When you execute this code, you will also find that if the robot is too close to the wall, that it will run in reverse.

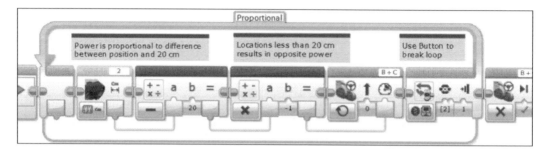

4. You may have also noticed that the robot moves very slowly as it approaches the stopping point. The reason we have used a button is to break the loop if the movement is excruciatingly slow. You can change this code by adding "gain" to the algorithm. If you multiply the difference by a larger factor, it will approach the stopping point quicker. When you execute this code, you will find that if you increase the gain too much, it will overshoot the stopping point and reverse direction. We can adjust these values using the `Advanced Math` block. We can type in any simple math function we need as shown in the next screenshot. In this block, the value of **a** is the measured position, **b** is the desired position, and **c** is the gain. The following equation can be seen in the next screenshot inside the `Advanced Math` block:

$$Power = -c \times (a - b)$$

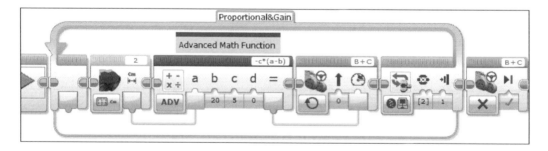

5. We can also define the desired stopping position and using variables. We can create two variable blocks called Gain and Location. We can write the value 5 to the Gain variable block and 20 to the Location variable block. Inside our loop, we can then read these variables and take the output of the Read Variable block and draw data wires into the Advanced Math block.

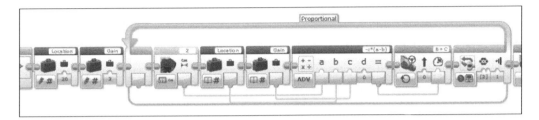

6. We can now select all the code we have written and make it into a MyBlock called Proportional. In this case, our MyBlock is going to be more advanced than before. We are going to add two parameters to the MyBlock. This will allow us to control the gain and location variables. This is shown in the following screenshot:

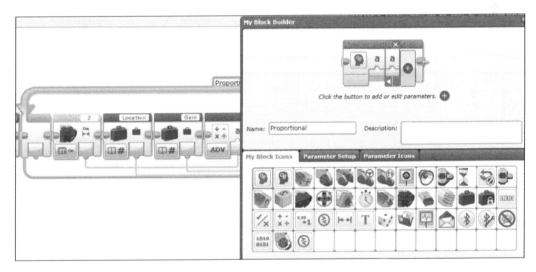

7. When creating the parameters, they should be set up for input values. We can define default values, such as 20 cm for the location and 3 for the gain as shown in the following screenshot:

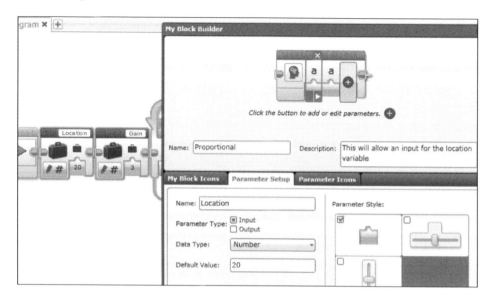

8. We can also select icons to represent these parameters so we know which one is the location parameter, and which one is the gain parameter:

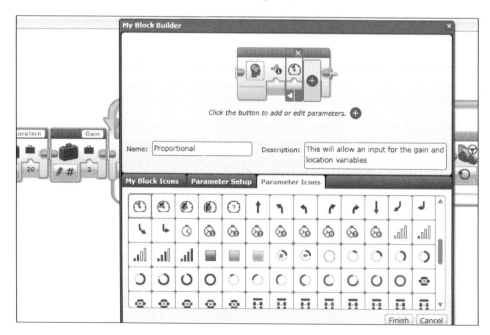

9. When you look at this MyBlock in the code, you can now change the values of the stopping location and gain by clicking on the parameter. We can also find the MyBlock in our collection of Programming blocks as shown in the following screenshot:

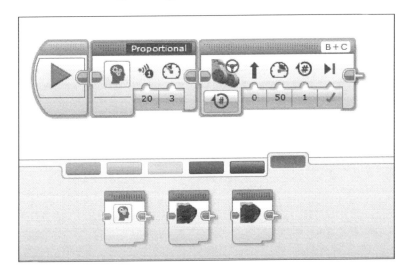

10. Before we execute the code, you need to open up the MyBlock one more time by clicking on it. When it opens up, we need to draw data wires from the parameters to the `Write Variable` blocks as shown in the following screenshot:

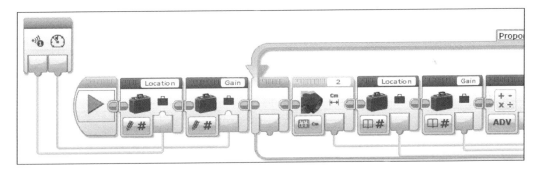

How it works...

The basic idea of the proportional algorithm is that the degree of correction needed is proportional to the error. So when our measured value is far from our goal, a large correction is applied. When our measured value is near our goal, only a small correction is applied. The algorithm also allows for over-corrections. Depending on what you are trying to do, you will need to play around with various values for the gain variable. If the gain is too large, you will overshoot your goal and oscillate around it. If your gain is too small, you will never reach your goal. Thinking back to the previous recipe, you can see how much better it would be if we used a proportional algorithm to zero in on a correct heading with the gyro sensor. The response time of the microprocessor also affects the efficiency of the algorithm. You can experiment by inserting a `Wait` block into the loop and see how this affects the behavior of the robot.

There's more...

Rather than adjusting the values of the gain and stopping location using the computer, we are going to write a program that will allow us to adjust these values on the brick itself.

Changing the Gain parameter

Using the buttons on the EV3 brick, we are going to select the value for the gain. We are going to write a program which has a `Switch` block and a loop to select the gain. First, we need to display commands on the EV3 screen. You can only program one line of text at a time, so it will take four `Display` block commands to give the relevant information to the user. Notice that only the first `Display` block has the Erase input checked and that the other `Display` blocks having the **y** inputs with greater values so that the wording does not overlap. Next, there is a `Brick Button Wait` block followed by writing to a variable block called `NewGain` which we will set to 0. This is illustrated in the following screenshot:

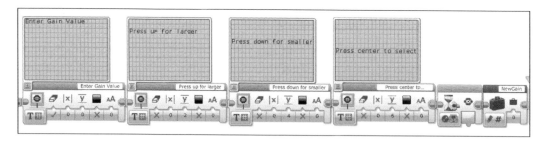

After defining the variable `NewGain`, we create an infinite loop block called `Enter Gain`. This is an example of when knowing the title of the `Loop` block is important. Later, we will write an interrupt for this loop and call it by name. Inside the loop there is a `Switch` block with four `case` structures which will be determined by the Brick Buttons. When you create a `Switch` block it defaults to two `case` structures and you can add extras. We will look at the details of the code closer in tabbed mode. This `Switch` block is going to allow us to increase or decrease the value of the `NewGain` variable.

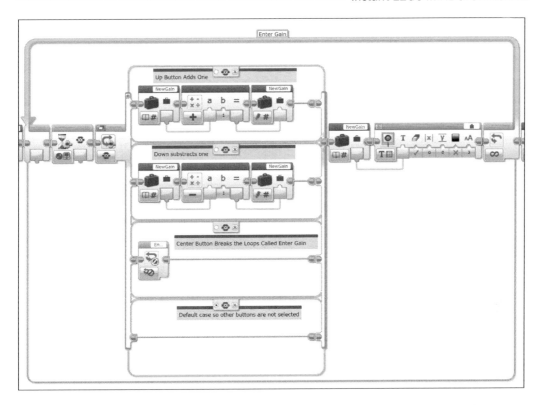

Before the switch there is a `Brick Button Wait` block. This wait block is waiting for a change in the state of the buttons. Without this wait block, when you press a button and continue to hold the button, the loop will run (and select the case of that button) for as long as the button is held. The initial wait block forces you to only progress through the loop once per push of the button. If you wanted to create an input where you would quickly scroll through numbers, you would not need this wait block. After the Switch, the value of the variable block is displayed on the screen. In the first case structure, which is selected by the Up brick button, the `NewGain` variable block is read, 1 is added to its value, and the variable is re-written with this increased value. This is illustrated in the following screenshot:

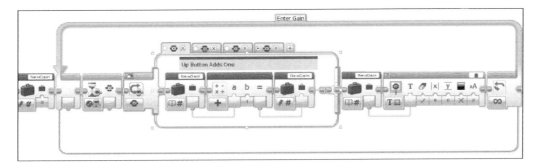

In the second case structure, selected by the Down brick button, the NewGain variable is read, 1 is subtracted from its value, and the variable is re-written. This is illustrated in the following screenshot:

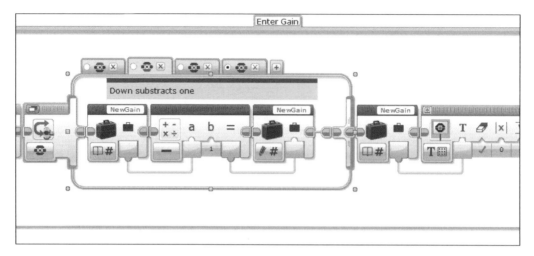

The third case structure, which is chosen by the center button, is responsible for breaking the loop. This contains a loop interrupt block which breaks the loop called Enter Gain and moves the program past this loop. This is illustrated in the following screenshot:

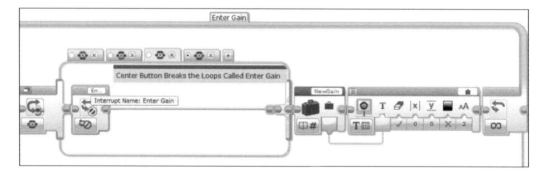

Because the Switch is inside of a loop, we actually need a default `case` that we do not plan to use. If we chose one of the other cases as the default, it would choose that case every other iteration of the loop. This is illustrated in the following screenshot:

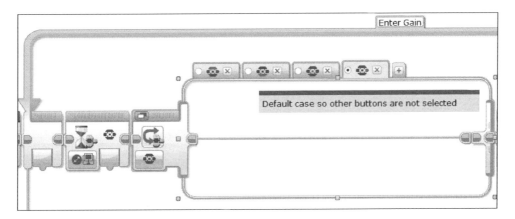

You can run this program as it is to select a number for the gain value. However, as we have created some complex code, this is an excellent opportunity to simplify things with a MyBlock. This time, we want our MyBlock to have one **Output** parameter. This is illustrated in the following screenshot:

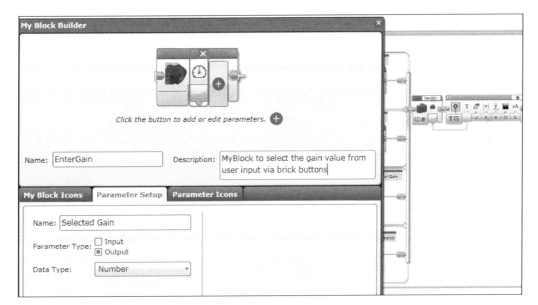

After you have created the MyBlock, you will need to draw a wire connecting the `NewGain Read Variable` block to the `Output` parameter. This is illustrated in the following screenshot:

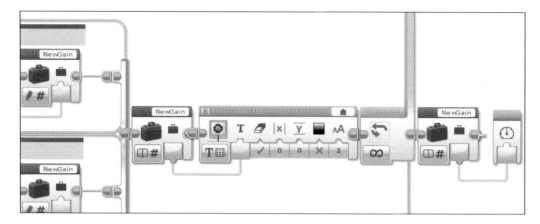

We can now write a simple program using just two MyBlocks that will control our robot. The `Enter Gain` Myblock will allow us to select a value for the gain on the brick. Execute this program and try various values of gain. This is illustrated in the following screenshot:

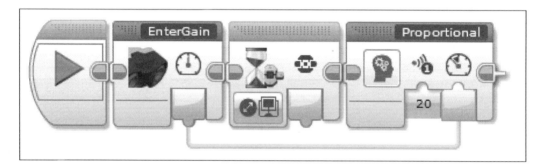

Changing the stopping distance

We are now going to go through a similar process to select a stopping distance on the EV3 brick.

You will start out by writing some similar code with a change in the words in the `Display` blocks and the name of the variable. Our `Variable` block is now called `Distance`. The starting value for the distance is 30 cm. This is illustrated in the following screenshot:

Again, we have created a Switch with four choices. I have written the code to increase the distance by 1, but you could easily use a larger number. This is illustrated in the following screenshot:

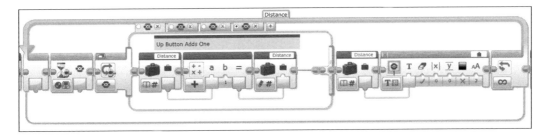

Likewise, the second `case` subtracts from the value of the `Distance` variable as shown in the following screenshot:

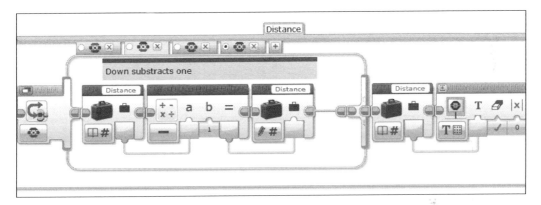

This time, the `Loop Interrupt` block sends a signal to interrupt the `Loop` called Distance. The fourth case will be the same as the Gain Switch. This is illustrated in the following screenshot:

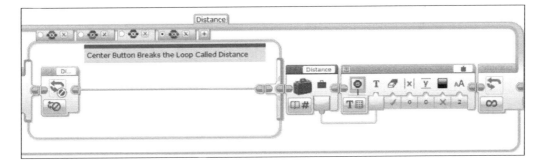

When we create the MyBlock this time, we should use an Output Parameter Icon which implies that we have selected a distance. This is illustrated in the following screenshot:

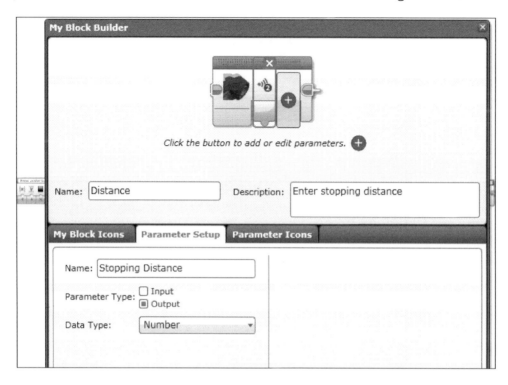

Again, we must make sure we connect the Output parameter by a wire to the Read Distance variable block as shown in the following screenshot:

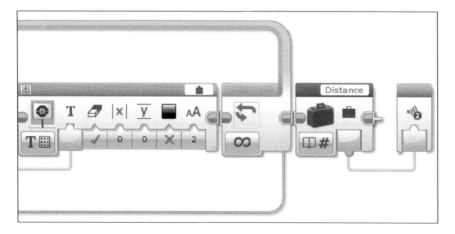

Now, when we write a master program, we will be able to select both the distance and the gain on the EV3 brick. Here we have a seemingly simple program with just a few blocks. Notice how we connect these blocks with wires:

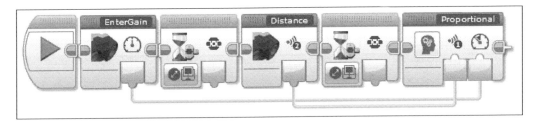

Saving data to files

In this previous recipe, instead of entering the stopping distance with the brick buttons, we are going to use the motion sensor to select the stopping distance with a separate program. We will then save the data to a file on EV3, and read the file into our motion program. First we will use Display blocks to tell the user to place the robot in the desired stopping location and push a button as shown in the following screenshot:

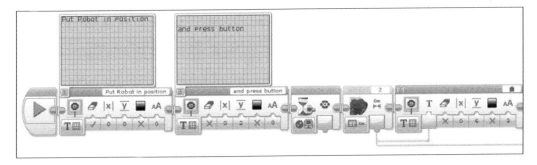

Next, a reading from the motion sensor is displayed on the screen. We will also write this motion sensor value to a file we will call `distance`. The output of the `Motion Sensor` block is connected by a wire to the `Write File` block. Before we write to the file, we initialize the file by deleting any information which may have been there before with the `Delete File` block. After we have written the information, we need to close the file using the `Close File` block. This is illustrated in the following screenshot:

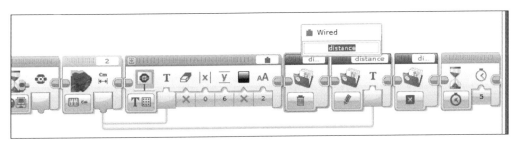

After we run this program we can write a second program to read the file from the EV3 brick. We can take the output of a Read File block and send it to a Display block as shown in the following screenshot:

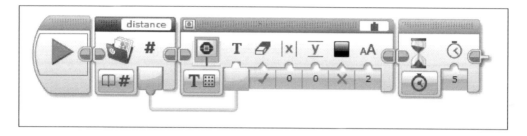

Now that we know how to read and write a file, we can combine what we have learned to use this in our main program. The following program allows us to enter the gain on the EV3 brick, but read the stopping distance from a file on the EV3. Wires will then send these two variables into the Proportional MyBlock as shown in the following screenshot:

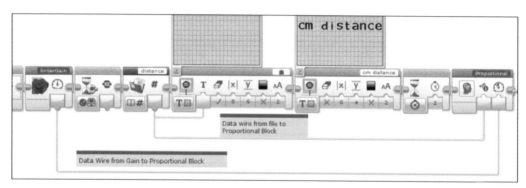

Proportional line follower (Advanced)

In this recipe, you will make a robot that will track a line quickly. The robot will be able to follow a line which makes corners sharper than 90 degrees using a proportional line follower.

Getting ready

First, you will need to build an attachment to hold the color sensor onto the robot.

Insert an axle that is five modules long into the color sensor. Place bushings onto the axle on either side of the sensor. This is illustrated in the following figure:

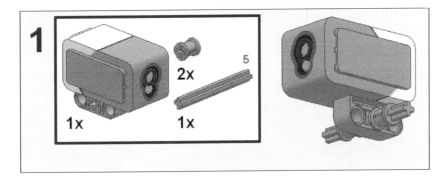

Attach the two-pin one-axle cross blocks onto the axle outside the bushings. This is illustrated in the following figure:

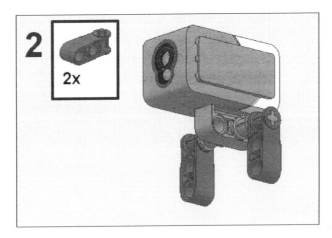

Insert 3-module pins into the cross blocks as shown in the following figure:

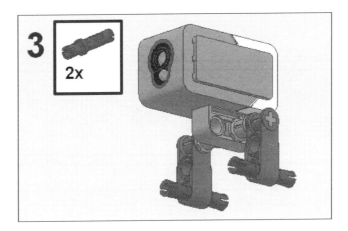

The pins will attach to the robot just in front of the castor. The bottom of the color sensor should be approximately leveled with the plastic part of the castor holder. If you are on a flat hard surface, your light sensor will be half a centimeter above the ground. If you are on a soft surface, you may need to add a spacer to raise up the sensor. This is illustrated in the following figure:

How to do it...

We are going to write a proportional line following code similar to the code used for the ultrasonic motion sensor.

1. We will write the following code:

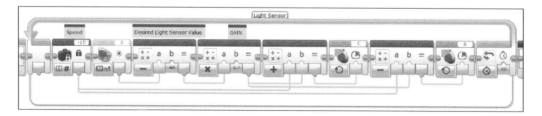

2. This program contains a loop so the robot will track a line for 30 seconds.

3. The base speed of the robot is controlled by a constant value which in this case, is 15.

4. You will need to determine a desired light sensor value for the robot to track on. You can either read the light sensor reading directly on your EV3 brick, or look at the panel on the lower-right hand corner of your screen. You should see all of the motors and sensors that are currently plugged into your brick. In the following screenshot, the current light sensor reading is **16**.

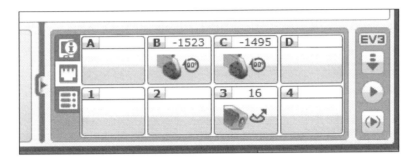

5. When tracking a line, you actually want to track on the edge of a line. Our code is designed to track on the right edge of a black line on a white surface. The line doesn't have to be black (or a white surface), but the stronger the contrast the better. One way to determine the desired light sensor value would be to place the light sensor on the edge of the line.

6. Alternatively, you could take two separate readings on the bright surface and the dark surface and take the average value.

7. In the code we discussed, the average value is 40, but you will have to determine the values which work in your own environment. Not only will the surfaces affect the value, but ambient room light can alter this value.

8. The code next finds the difference between the desired value and the sensor reading.

9. This difference is multiplied by a gain factor, which for the optical proportional line follower will probably be between 0 and 1. In this program, I chose a gain of 0.7.

10. The result is added to the base speed of one motor and subtracted from the based speed of the other motor:

$$MotorBPower = Speed - Gain \times (LightSensor - DesiredValue)$$

$$MotorCPower = Speed + Gain \times (LightSensor - DesiredValue)$$

11. After taking the light sensor readings, practice with several numbers to figure out the best speeds and proportionality constants to make your robot follow a line.

How it works...

This algorithm will make corrections to the path of the robot based on how far off from the line the robot is. It determines this by calculating the difference between the light sensor reading and the value of the light sensor reading on the edge. Each wheel of the robot rotates at a different speed proportional to how far from the line it is. There is a base speed for each wheel and then they will go either slower or faster for a smooth turning. You will find that a large gain value will be needed for sharp turns, but the robot will tend to overcorrect and wobble when it is following a straight line. A smaller gain and higher speed can work effectively when the line is relatively straight or follows a gradual curve. The most important factor to determine is the desired light sensor value.

Although your color sensor can detect several colors, we will not be using that feature in this program. The color sensor included in your kit emits red light and we are measuring the reflection of that reflected light. The height of the sensor above the floor is critical, and there is a sweet spot for line tracking at about half a centimeter above the floor. The light comes out of the sensor in a cone. You want the light reflected into the sensor to be as bright as possible, so if your sensor is too high, the reflected intensity will be weaker. Assuming your color sensor is pointing straight down at the floor (as it is in our robot design), then you will see a circular red spot on the floor. Because the distance between the detector and the light emitter is about 5 to 6 mm, the diameter of this circle should be about 11 mm across. If the circle is large, then your color sensor is too high and the intensity will weaken. If the circle is smaller than this, then the sensor will not pick up the emitted light.

The color sensor in the LEGO MINDSTORMS EV3 kit is different from the optical sensors included in the earlier LEGO NXT kits. Depending on your application, you might want to pick up some of the older NXT lights and color sensors. The light sensor in the NXT 1.0 kit could not detect color and only measured reflected intensity of a red LED. What is good about this sensor is that it will actually work flush against the surface and saves the need to calibrate changes due to the ambient lighting conditions. The color sensor in the NXT 2.0 kit actually emitted colored lights and contained a general photo detector. However, it did not directly measure color, but measured the reflection of colored light, which it would emit. This actually allowed you to track along different colored lines, but it was also slower. The new EV3 sensor detects colors directly, works quickly, and emits only red light.

There's more...

How can you adjust the algorithm to adjust the response of the robot to follow the line faster or smoother, depending on the shape of the line without needing to change your program?

Entering the parameters using buttons

We will use several MyBlocks to allow us to enter values for the light sensor reading, gain, and speed right on the robot. We will also have a separate MyBlock for a modified Proportional Tracker code. After you have first written the MyBlocks, you can write the following code to track a line. This is illustrated in the following screenshot:

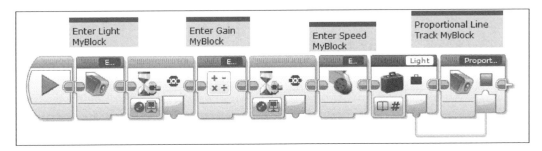

The first MyBlock will allow us to enter a value for the light reading. This MyBlock is similar to what we wrote in the previous recipe for entering a value on the brick. Notice that in the display we ask the reader for a Light value, and the variable is now called `Light`. A starting value of 30 will probably be a good edge sensor reading for most applications.

The loop is now called `Enter Light`. For the case structure containing `Loop Interrupt`, make sure it refers to the correct Loop. Also, notice all of the variables we refer to are called `Light`. This is illustrated in the following screenshot:

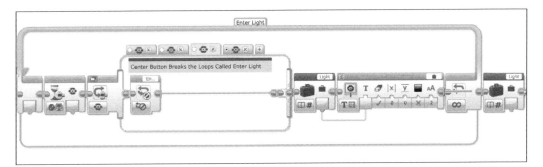

Using increments of 1 to increase or decrease the light sensor value will still work:

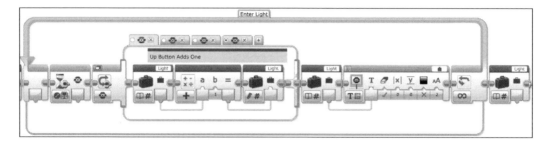

In the next screenshot, you can better see how the Down button subtracts 1 from the value of the variable:

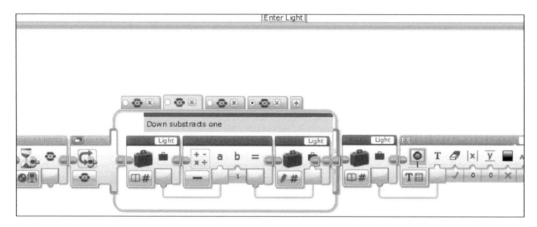

Do not forget that our `Switch` still needs a fourth `case` structure for the default value. This is illustrated in the following screenshot:

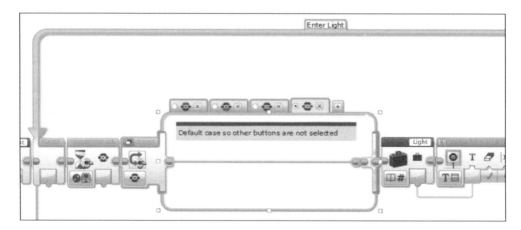

You will write a similar MyBlock for entering a gain value. Note that the names of the variables are different as are the names of the loops and `Loop Interrupt`. Also, for this MyBlock it is appropriate to increase or decrease the gain multiplier by one tenth. This is illustrated in the following screenshot:

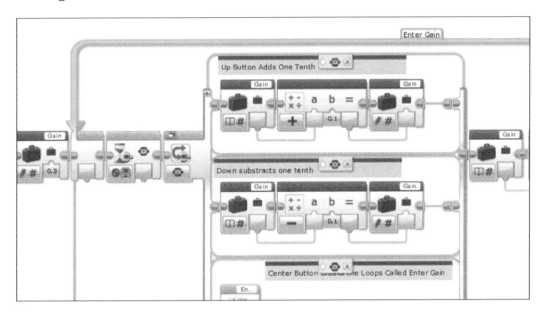

The third MyBlock for this program will select the seed. Again, remember the change in the variables and loop names. This is illustrated in the following screenshot:

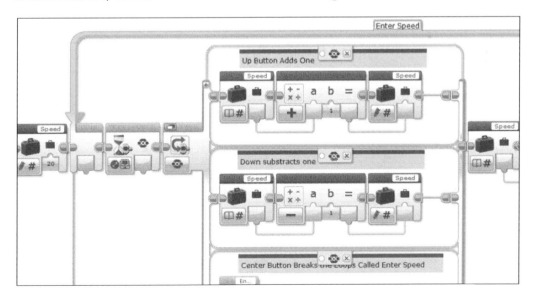

The `Proportional` MyBlock is a bit more complex than the code we wrote at the beginning of this recipe. In our program at the beginning of this recipe, if you wanted to change a light value, you had to change it in the computer program itself. The MyBlock will accept the Light variable from an external parameter which will be useful later in this recipe. The new program will allow you to change light values using the EV3 brick buttons. We now find the difference between the light sensor reading and the external parameter defined by our desired light reading. This difference is multiplied by the `Gain` variable. We then add or subtract this to/ from the `Speed` variable. The next screenshot has the first five commands in this loop:

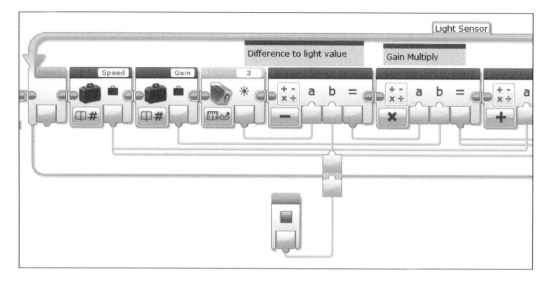

The next screenshot has the remaining commands in this loop where the values are sent to the motor blocks:

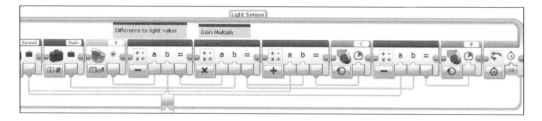

Calibrating the light sensor values

Now are going to calibrate the robot by placing the robot on the edge of line and saving that information to a file. Create a MyBlock from the following code. This takes a light sensor reading and saves it to the file `light`.

Now our main program contains this new MyBlock. Instead of reading the light variable, it reads the value stored in the file as illustrated in the next screenshot:

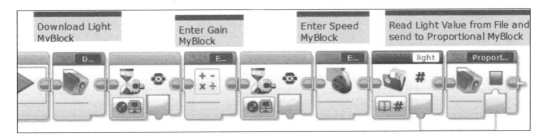

Increased accuracy in light calibration

The program in the *Calibrating the light sensor values* section assumes you have your robot placed right on the edge of the line. Alternatively, we could take calibration readings on the bright and dark areas. In the following MyBlock, the readings from two measurements are averaged. This means you will have to move the robot around by hand. This is illustrated in the following screenshot:

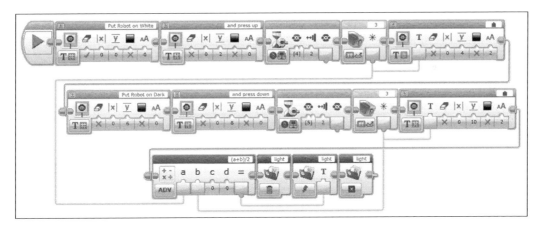

Our main program now takes the average value created by this new MyBlock and feeds it to the Proportional Controller.

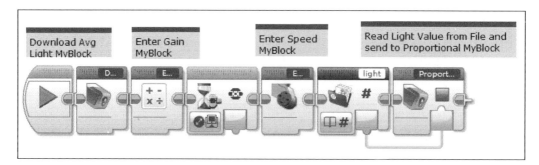

In this recipe, you have learned to develop a proportional line controller using one light sensor. Without changing the code, using buttons on the robot you can change the execution parameters. An additional challenge could be to have the robot rotate and scan for these two values. You could also use more than one light sensor.

Thank you for buying
Instant LEGO MINDSTORMS EV3

About Packt Publishing

Packt, pronounced 'packed', published its first book "*Mastering phpMyAdmin for Effective MySQL Management*" in April 2004 and subsequently continued to specialize in publishing highly focused books on specific technologies and solutions.

Our books and publications share the experiences of your fellow IT professionals in adapting and customizing today's systems, applications, and frameworks. Our solution based books give you the knowledge and power to customize the software and technologies you're using to get the job done. Packt books are more specific and less general than the IT books you have seen in the past. Our unique business model allows us to bring you more focused information, giving you more of what you need to know, and less of what you don't.

Packt is a modern, yet unique publishing company, which focuses on producing quality, cutting-edge books for communities of developers, administrators, and newbies alike. For more information, please visit our website: www.packtpub.com.

Writing for Packt

We welcome all inquiries from people who are interested in authoring. Book proposals should be sent to author@packtpub.com. If your book idea is still at an early stage and you would like to discuss it first before writing a formal book proposal, contact us; one of our commissioning editors will get in touch with you.

We're not just looking for published authors; if you have strong technical skills but no writing experience, our experienced editors can help you develop a writing career, or simply get some additional reward for your expertise.

C Programming for Arduino

ISBN: 978-1-84951-758-4   Paperback: 512 pages

Learn how to program and use Arduino boards with series of engaging examples, illustrating each core concept

1. Use Arduino boards in your own electronic hardware & software projects

2. Sense the world by using several sensory components with your Arduino boards

3. Create tangible and reactive interfaces with your computer

4. Discover a world of creative wiring and coding fun!

Unity 4.x Game AI Programming

ISBN: 978-1-84969-340-0   Paperback: 232 pages

Learn and implement game AI in Unity3D with a lot of sample projects and next-generation techniques to use in your Unity3D projects

1. A practical guide with step-by-step instructions and example projects to learn Unity3D scripting

2. Learn pathfinding using A* algorithms as well as Unity3D pro features and navigation graphs

3. Implement finite state machines (FSMs), path following, and steering algorithms

Please check **www.PacktPub.com** for information on our titles

CryENGINE 3 Game Development: Beginner's Guide

ISBN: 978-1-84969-200-7   Paperback: 354 pages

Discover how to use the CryENGINE 3 free SDK, the next-generation, real-time game development tool

1. Begin developing your own games of any scale by learning to harness the power of the Award Winning CryENGINE® 3 game engine

2. Build your game worlds in real-time with CryENGINE® 3 Sandbox as we share insights into some of the tools and features useable right out of the box.

3. Harness your imagination by learning how to create customized content for use within your own custom games through the detailed asset creation examples within the book.

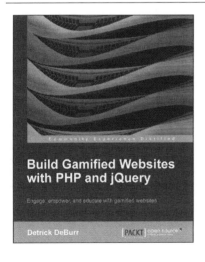

Build Gamified Websites with PHP and jQuery

ISBN: 978-1-78216-811-9   Paperback: 124 pages

Engage, empower, and educate with gamified websites

1. Build your own Gamified website

2. Use game mechanics to motivate the users

3. Understand and implement game design process

Please check **www.PacktPub.com** for information on our titles